Verse Cycles

Caroline Burrows

JAWBONE
Words to keep you talking

British Library Cataloguing in Publication Data
A catalogue record is available on request from the British Library.

ISBN 978-1-7392932-4-6

Cover illustration: Caroline Burrows
Layout and page setting by Wessex Media
Editors: Clare Morris, Peter Roe, Izzy Robertson
All images copyright Caroline Burrows, all rights reserved.

Jawbone illustration - Mary Anning

Printed and bound by
Blackmore Limited
Longmead, Shaftesbury, Dorset. SP7 8PX

FSC
www.fsc.org
FSC® C008152

The mark of
responsible forestry

The Blackmore Group is committed to the concept of reducing to a minimum any actions that have an adverse effect on the environment. It supports this commitment by operating both to the ISO 9001:2015 Quality Management System and the ISO 14001:2015 Environmental Management System. In conducting its printing business it aims to prevent pollution and to save natural resource by operating in the most environmentally efficient and friendly way and by recycling wherever this is practical. This it does by not only keeping its use of materials down to a minimum but also its use of non-renewable resources such as petrol and, indirectly, of electricity. Furthermore it aims in its printing business to encourage its customers to adopt environmentally friendly business practices wherever possible.

Poets have much in common with fairies.

Thank you to all those who believed,
without you,
this wouldn't exist.

Introduction

"Voice," as William Sieghart* observes, "is the holy grail for emerging poets." It is an aspect of Caroline Burrows' poetry that is immediately apparent. Whether read or heard, her voice has a compelling quality that communicates with engaging clarity across time, place and experience. When mixed with detailed research and an assured understanding of poetic form in all its intricacies, it makes for a deliciously intoxicating cocktail. Poetry for Caroline is as much part of what she is as what she does. She writes poetry with elegant assurance but, more than this, she lives by the beliefs she explores in her poems. Her most recent poetry tour involved cycling from Bristol to Berwick-upon-Tweed, through storm and heatwave, with her belongings stashed away in bulging panniers: a clear reflection of her steely resolve.

It is astonishing to realise that this is her first collection, given the grand sweep of her understanding of the poetic genre and her expertise within it. *Verse Cycles,* as the title suggests, invites us to delight in the journey as well as the destination; there are plenty of side roads to discover as, at Caroline's subtle prompting, we retrace our steps to admire the view from a different perspective. I am immensely proud to introduce Caroline's collection. She is a remarkable poet of talent, heart, scholarship and understanding. Enjoy the journey!

Clare Morris (Dr)
Exeter Slam Champion 2022
Author of *Devon Maid Walking*
February 2024

*Sieghart, W. (2024). 'Preface' in The Forward Book of Poetry 2024.
London: Forward Prizes for Poetry

Acknowledgements

'A Hundred Years after Wilfred Owen's 'Futility': For the Statue in Birkenhead' - first published in The Wilfred Owen Association Journal Volume 2, 2020; and subsequently online by the Rainbow Poems: Remembrance 2020.

'Ashes to Ashes: Nature Knows No Bounds' selected for The University of Exeter's Festival of Compassion 2021. First published in First Flight: Paper Cranes Anthology 2023; and subsequently in Morecambe Poetry Festival 2023 Anthology.

'A Sonnet for Triodos' - first published online by Triodos: The Ethical Bank 2022.

'Heartbroken and Hungover in Oxfam Books and Music' - first published online by The Charles Causley Trust 2022.

'I Heard a Bird' - first published in First Flight: Paper Cranes Anthology 2023.

'Junkies in the Underpass' - first published online by Bristol Ideas 2018.

'The Body of Water in the Bath' - first published in Sinew: Ten Years of Poetry in the Brew 2021.

'The Death of Chatterton's Romanticised Suicide' - first published online by Glenside Hospital Museum/Bristol Ideas 2021.

'The Only Way Out is to Cycle Through' - first published online by the Janet Coates Memorial Prize 2021.

'Tintern Abbey' - first published online by The Traditional Cycle Shop when Poet in Residence 2022.

'Tomato' - first published online by Tomato Art Fest 2022.

Follow the QR code to watch the documentary - *Bristol Bike Bard*. (2021). Directed by Dave MacFarlane. U.K. DMTwo Media.

CONTENTS

Photo © Dave MacFarlane
from the documentary 'Bristol Bike Bard'

Junkies in the Underpass

Below St Philips Causeway, Bristol

I cycle quickly past
The junkies in the underpass.
Their dealer stands dead centre,
A white man dressed in black,
Astride a bike with no lights,
This underworld, his stage.

"*Evenin'!*" brays this king,
Of short sharp pricks,
As I ride wide of him,
Peddling his shit,
To two locals laid low,
Between the broken glass and grit.

His shout carries a glint,
Like the water in the bottle,
And the tarnished metal spoon,
I spy left at pedal level,
A scene waning,
Like the moon.

Yellow light reveals them huddled,
Beneath the underpass' mosaics,
Which depict a long history,
Of most of Bristol's trades,
This current exchange excluded,
And the sugar, and the slaves.

Graffiti scrawls across the pictures,
Letters and words all strung out,
Not street art,
Not a Banksy,
Just a public place defaced.

It's an update, representing,
This exact time and space.

Finding my Flow in Fishponds

(sestina)

In a steady stream of cyclists I flow.
At Fishponds, I leave the Bristol Bike Path,
Pedalling where neon outshines sunlight,
On a road that crawls to a stagnant stop,
Where unparked cars on a tarmac river
Exhale moist splutters of phlegm as they breathe.

There are puddles but no ponds. Did fish breathe
Here, once upon a time before this overflow
Of crazed paving on this toxic river?
Its only banks: cash machines on the path
By stuck drivers, surging, queuing non-stop,
To rage at yet another traffic light.

Pigeons eat chucked fried chicken, then take flight:
Grey plumes flapping in the grey smog they breathe.
A tired man fumes at a lying bus stop,
To a screeched horn chorus in constant flow.
I get off and walk my bike on the path,
These are not safe lanes for a non-driver.

Life doesn't thrive on this ersatz river,
Between billboards, thin cracks form a skylight,
I turn that way to a less travelled path,
Congestion eases, blue skies start to breathe
Above garden parked cars, which I follow
To a dead end where bikes don't need to stop.

At Oldbury Court, it's the greys that stop.
Greens grow on trees on a green grass river,
There's only one van, where ice-cream cones flow,
Its machines thrum as kids squeal round its light,
Joggers plod, plod, plod, panting as they breathe,
And we weave round each other on the path.

Fresh mud and leaves soften that hardened path,
And the trees take over. They're retreats: top -
Homes for birds and squirrels to live and breathe
Off-grid lives near the Frome, a real river.
I freewheel down, me and my bike feel light,
Gravity guides the water I follow.

On the path beside the giggling river,
I stop to watch trees dance in dappled light,
And the breeze whispers, "Breathe, go with our flow."

Scan this QRCode with your
smartphone to watch a recording
of this poem read by the author.

Photo © Dave MacFarlane
from the documentary 'Bristol Bike Bard'

Solar Sonnet 8
All Under One Sun

In Scottish Gaelic, it is called *grian*,
The word was *sunne* in Middle English,
Rā is Maori, that's antipodean,
In Middle Earth, say *anar*, if Elvish.
It can turn the heads of young sunflowers,
Gets followed by the faces of daisies,
It heats air and creates thundershowers,
And helps tides spring high with the waves on seas,
Without it, our world would have no more days,
At night we'd never ever see the Moon,
Just specks of light would shine as we stargaze,
From memories of suns, out past Neptune,
Would Proxima Centauri greet exiles,
If we drifted twenty-five trillion miles?

Ashes to Ashes
Nature Knows No Bounds

(Spenserian stanza)

Your thin bare arms are bent at the elbows,
As your wave welcomes the migrant starlings,
Fingers beckoning: "Rest here, perch in rows."
Fallen leaves replaced with warm feathered wings,
Bitter squalls shushed by the birds' chatterings,
You're rooted in concord with avians.
The birds lift as one: unified beings,
Your seeds fly free in spinning rotations,
And ash saplings greet starlings for generations.

A Wilfred Owen Odyssey
A Spring Cycling Offensive

My bike's fully loaded, my own pack-mule,
A pilgrimage of Wilfred Owen poetry,
Riding south between the Pennines and the Irish Sea,
I set my sights for distant Liverpool.
"You can't miss it," says a man I ask for directions,
Casting his curse, I get lost different ways,
'Til I skirt Leyland where tanks were once made,
I'm relieved I've survived it through Preston.

Spring lambs bounce around flat fields in the Ribble,
Near two crows ganging up on a baby squirrel,
The B-road takes me over six screaming lanes,
To a Scouse bus honking with offensive disdain.
In Birkenhead, a statue called 'Futility'
Shows a man with his head in his hands who's sat,
With a wreath of paper poppies in his lap.
The bronze remains dull although it's sunny.

Expecting a veteran, I meet a musician,
Who went to the B.I., Wilfred's old school:
Only a wall remains where a cruel
Head caned kids for breaking archaic rules.
In his Wilfmobile, he shows me locations:
"Did you know a dead famous poet lived there?"
The people living inside couldn't care.
Then it's back to the Wilfred Owen Museum,
Hearing how he's adapted poetic rhythm,
Into a Wilfred Owen musical.

Near Chester, I rest in a cyclists' café,
Where a roadie shows me a safer greenway,
Past a cemetery where rows of soldiers fill
Uniform graves standing to attention.

Despite the forecast there's miles of cold wet stuff,
But *Warm Showers* greet me at Oswestry
From members of that cycling community.
There's Wilf's birthplace, another statue, an exhibition,
A plaque, a park, and the church where he prayed,
A Wilfred lemon and poppy seed cake was made
By the librarian. Second place. In a Bake Off.

I wait by a country field as cows are unloaded,
One runs bellowing; it's separated;
In another truck is its baby calf.
It's quieter when I reach city grass outside
Shrewsbury Abbey: whose bells when they were ringing
War's end, that's when Wilfred's mum got news he'd died.

At a pub B&B, I stop cycling,
In the bath, the acoustics sound great being read,
Wilfred Owen by Richard Burton
On YouTube before bed.

A Hundred Years After Wilfred Owen's 'Futility'
For the Statue in Birkenhead

Put the soldier's statue,
On a corner, opposite the square.
Named like the poem: 'Futility'
Sits near the cenotaph that keeps score,
Of those who were lost in battles won.
All the statue can do today is warn:
War games aren't played for fun.

Shake hands politicians,
For honouring the heroes who die.
Their blood turns black your profit-margins
When you sell arms for the M.O.D.
Is it for this war-machine we mourn
Their blown arms, their left legs, their right minds,
And fake poppies get worn?

The statue by Jim Whelan represents a WWI soldier. It was erected following years of campaigning after local playing fields dedicated to those killed in the War were sold off for housing. The statue features Wilfred Owen's poem 'Futility' on a plaque. I used the original poem as a model for the structure of mine.

A Kyrielle for a Pipistrelle

(kyrielle)

A Durham Cathedral choir,
Sing notes only heard by higher
Beings on their own camino,
For whom faith involves letting go.

In the home of the hereafter,
Where sandstone meets wooden rafter,
Safe havens hallowed though hollow,
House those with the faith to let go.

They gather their congregation,
Every day for contemplation,
In the Cloisters as Vespers flow,
Readying their faith to let go.

Each small Odin in robed vestment,
Hangs its head for enlightenment,
Knowing that the end of day's glow,
Arrives with faith in letting go.

As the light turns crepuscular,
Forms merge sacred and secular,
The choir of chiropterans show,
They all have faith. They all let go.

Round and round the Cloisters they sing,
Black shadows fleeting, fluttering,
Their hymns beyond what humans know,
With faith their own way, they let go.

Except one's landed, unfounded,
Its world's downside-up and grounded,
A pup's wrong location-echo,
Has lost faith in where it should go.

But healing hands lift the pup up,
Blue medical gloves envelop,
It in hues its eyes do not know,
Faith exhausted, it won't let go.

It clings to fingers paternal,
Which encourage flight supernal,
But the bat gives its silent no,
It's lost faith in how to let go.

Our group makes its own Kyrielle
Eleison for the pipistrelle,
Sung for the bat pup in limbo,
Please, give it the faith to let go.

Misguided, for now, it holds on,
As our unanswered orison,
Leaves us incommunicado,
In good faith, we can't let it go.

In this sanctuary of earthlings,
Sequestered, the maternal wings,
Knows all their hands link to help grow,
Faith in the act of letting go.

The bat is placed for safekeeping,
In a box to rest while sleeping,
'Til it rehears voices alto,
Sing with their faith soaring, let go.

In the same Cloisters, the next week,
One tiny bat's shadow, I seek,
I find as above, so below,
And keep the faith that it let go.

*Durham Cathedral is home to the second largest colony of Common Pipistrelle bats in the UK. The staff are trained in Bat First Aid. I saw the bats when I was performing and teaching poetry as part of the Cathedral's Gaia/Earth installation.

Heartbroken and Hungover
In Oxfam Books and Music

Heartbroken and hungover in Oxfam,
Neither are safe states to be in,
Amongst the shelves where I bought you that book,
The one about guitars and zen.

I browse what's now called pre-loved poetry,
While a song makes me feel tortured,
Donated Juliet is in Dire Straits,
Everything in here's unwanted.

I find a napkin in my bag, just in case,
The rising tide of tears overflow,
As each book mocks me with cruel verses,
I read differently not long ago.

I fight the urge to rip out the pages,
Scrunch them up, and set them alight.
Such behaviour in a charity shop,
Might feel good, but wouldn't be right.

I scan for editions by Sylvia Plath,
None. Her works don't get regifted.
But two copies of Crow perch on the rows,
Ironic. Ted's get discarded.

To try and distract myself. To not cry,
On the napkin I write in a scrawl,
'Cos the notebook you gave me with roses on,
I shut out of sight in a drawer.

Back home, I transfer this into that notebook,
Poetic justice. Don't you think?
The dam breaks, the rose pages get watered,
And black petals are made from blurred ink.

Bike, Book, and Bench

I rest my bike on the bench in the middle,
The best of three overlooking the estuary.
Under the warm blanket of clouds covering the sun,
I open my book to read Sylvia's 'Yew Tree'.

Until a sharp pain from something so small,
Brings me back to real life's buzzing and biting.
I flick the insect away from its feast of my blood,
As a burning begins to spread from its sting.

The bench on my left has young love on display,
The man's arm staking claim over his woman's shoulder.
The other side watch a lone bird ride the currents,
They're much more sedate, about fifty years older.

I turn a fresh page to Yeats' rare mountain hare,
But again, I'm brought out of my reader's retreat,
By a group babbling towards sheep that are grazing
On salt marsh that adds flavour when they're made into meat.

The seats stay the same, the couples have changed,
At one, a man's accent is making me frown,
It's like the one my head's failing to silence.
There's no escape, in sleep, home, countryside, or town.

Breezes chase each other through the leaves and grass,
Even the trees stand in pairs, forever entrenched.
The bike waits to be ridden, the book lays unread,
Not alone, but all alone, I sit on this bench.

Tintern Abbey
Lines Composed Quite a Few Miles Away
at a Garden Centre in Chepstow

(blank verse)

I sought out Romantic enlightenment,
To create like Wordsworth a 'Spot of Time',
As writing 'Tintern Abbey' did for him,
Where his poem recorded a snapshot,
To think back on fondly in future times.

I studied Will's poem the night before
My first ride out with Bristol CTC,
Planning to cycle to that same Abbey.
Wild gothic images formed in my mind:
Me on a sublime epic adventure,
To ruins amongst lush dramatic hills.

The cyclists met at a water tower,
From England we battled cold driving rain,
Over the old Severn Bridge, winds joined us
Screaming through its two, huge, white, tuning-forks.
Once across, we sheltered in a tunnel,
In which a spray-painted cartoon dragon
Welcomed us to Wales: "*Croeso i Gymru*".

The bike club's big wigs held a committee:
Clawed, wet, gloved fingers were raised in favour;
Two abstained, only my digit against.
Tintern Abbey's ruins were abandoned,
The vote: visit Chepstow garden centre.

Potted plants framed that sanitised landscape,
Our soggy arses sat in its café.
I grumpily cradled a large latte,
Devoured a cherry and almond slice.

As we all warmed up, my mood lightened, too,
The seeds of new friendships germinated,
Opening up wider my narrow view.
The result: a 'spot of time' memory,
Surpassing academic pretensions.
Different roads to the same destination.

*I eventually made it to Tintern Abbey on a much sunnier day, and even stopped at the garden centre for a coffee on the way.

Chatterton
The Death of Chatterton's Romanticised Suicide

(Spenserian sonnet)

Thomas Chatterton's death is infamous,
Like Kurt Cobain's 'flame of glory' trigger,
Like Ms. Plath's sleeping gas to Morpheus,
The flowers floating with Ophelia.
Shakespeare wrote an exquisite cadaver,
But all are works of Romantic fiction,
Editing truths in case they disfigure
Mortals made martyrs of self-destruction.
The myth of Chatterton's expiration
Makes believe gifted minds are blessed and cursed,
Ill-fated towards a doomed conclusion,
That's a dangerous trope when left unversed.
It sustains but falsely diagnoses
Those shown in artfully framed death poses.

*Bristol born Thomas Chatterton died in 1770 in London aged 17. Sales accounts recorded by the apothecary indicate his cause of death, often believed to be by suicide, could possibly have been an accidental medication overdose. Henry Wallis' mid-19th century painting 'The Death of Chatterton' depicts a death scene in a manner this poem challenges, and was commissioned by Glenside Hospital, the Museum of Mental Health Care, and Bristol Ideas, when marking the 250th anniversary of Chatterton's death.

14

The Cromarty *Òran*

(Burns stanza)

Arms of land hug a safe harbour,
From Cromarty's South/*Deas* Sutor,
Tuath/North, they greet each other.
A mouth opens,
Grins a Gaelic welcome: *Fàilte,*
The Firth broadens.

On Ladies Walk, up from The Paye,
The snowdrops have arrived; they say,
"Winter to Spring, we've reached midway."
Their view brings cheer.
Là Fhèill Brìghde: St. Brigid's Day,
Imbolc is here!

Skulls and crossbones don't mortify,
On old grave slabs which do not lie,
They prompt, "Remember you must die,"
Their script's deadpan,
"*Memento mori,*" they all sigh,
Live while you can!

The Body of Water in the Bath

(pantoum)

I am contained within a body of water,
Under a face that ticks the way of its shadow,
A channel opens to ease stress on another,
One body is stopped from its anti-clockwise flow.

Under a face that ticks the way of its shadow,
Both bodies are held in a sort of suspension,
One body is stopped from its anti-clockwise flow,
As time starts to drift in the other direction.

Both bodies are held in a sort of suspension,
One circulates, one settles only to stagnate,
As time starts to drift in the other direction,
Gravity drags both back to the earth and adds weight.

One circulates, one settles only to stagnate,
A channel opens to ease stress on another,
Gravity drags both back to the earth and adds weight,
I am contained within a body of water.

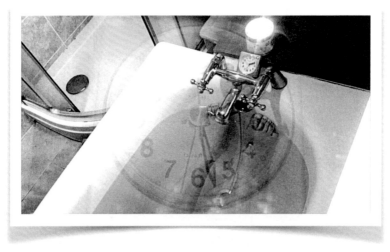

*During an episode of depression, I struggled with feeling physically sluggish. Hot
baths brought temporary relief, making me feel lighter until the plug was pulled.*

Half-Life
In the Dark with Anti-Depressant
and Other Types of Withdrawal

(villanelle)

I want to find my way to the river bed,
Far from glaring streetlights by a blazing window,
I want to lie down, under bright stars, long dead.

My phone's torch won't shine; energy's down in the red,
Confused constellations can't tell me where to go,
I can't find my way to the river bed.

A ghostly snowdrop hangs its troubled head,
The mean moon slivers from the Earth's shadow,
I want like to lie down, under bright stars, long dead.

Beams of light blind my lonely silhouette,
A white van stops driven by a man I know,
He won't let me find my way to the river bed.

I try to walk on, in fear where I tread,
The engine rumbles as the van and man follow,
I want to lie down, under bright stars, long dead.

He takes me home; says what he feels needs said,
My reduced anti-depressant dose is too low.
He brought me back from the edge near the river bed,
Stopped me laying down under bright stars, dead.

An acute depressive episode was triggered when trying to come off prescribed anti-depressants under medical guidance with a 50% reduction in the dose. Medical NICE guidelines have since been changed and advise slowly tapering due to the negative effects of withdrawal symptoms.

I Heard a Bird

I heard a bird,
But couldn't hear what it said,
My window was shut, I'd put my ears to bed.

My eyes swelled red,
When I saw the bee,
I closed the curtains, wondering how it stung me.

Rain dripped on my tongue,
From clouds in the ceiling,
I shut my mouth, it tasted of nothing.

I touched a hand,
My palm held something empty,
Which read like a book of futures too heavy.

That's when the spider
Crawled down my spine,
It hung from its rope. The end of the line.

A thought tried to form,
But dissolved in old air,
I was hermetically sealed from what was out there.

The bluebell in its glass,
With no hope of rebirth,
Forgot its fragrance, disconnected from earth.

The bird returned,
Pecked a crack, formed a skylight,
It sang,
"Just listen, you will be alright."

Solar Sonnet 11
Noctilucent

Our world view is so heliocentric,
The Sun's presence is felt by its absence,
A day that shines is more optimistic,
Grey clouds manifest a sadder sentence,
But summer's nightfall shows a magic cloud,
Its noctilucent, it glows in the dark,
Making the mesosphere look as if ploughed,
With silver sparkling from the low Sun's spark,
Light twinkles, it beams, and it even waves,
It travels in time in units of years,
Sunlight that shone on medieval knaves,
Has just reached Hydra's exoplanets' spheres,
Do their telescopes watch our light absorbed,
To spot if what circles our Sun is orbed?

Lost in Space
Our future has been written in the stars,
Seen by the Sun on a planet between us,
Yet still, humans race the heavens to Mars,
While turning Earth towards hell like Venus.

Resurrection
For the Unmarked Grave of a Woman Accused of Witchcraft

(luc bat)

Everyone thinks I'm dead,
Where I lay in my bed of earth,
Below thin skins of turf,
Unmarked, thought of no worth, my grave
Senses every shock wave
In this shallow enclave. I wait
To hear announced my fate:
Bury first, then cremate. I'm drowned
For good measure. My mound
Is slick with hell-bound salt-less tears,
Thundering, my fate nears,
All others shut their ears and run
From death, so quickly done,
A flash so fast to stun or fry,
Lightning strikes where I lie.
Strike! AGAIN! I defy. My earth,
Which all believed a dearth
Of life, stirs in rebirth. Heaven
Sends my resurrection
With bolts of nitrogen supplies,
Seed, roots, stem, leaves, I rise:
One tiny wildflower kissed by the skies.

*I cycled the 1612 Lancashire Witch Trials route. Most of the women and men executed weren't given proper graves. Separately, in nearby Woodplumpton, a boulder prevents Meg Shelton, the Fylde Witch, rising from hers. Wildflowers were growing around the edge of the stone when I visited. I like to think you can't keep a good woman down.

Solar Sonnet 1
The Spring Equinox

At noon, Earth's star shone due south in the sky:
A solar compass on the equinox,
It crossed the Cusp of Aries, reaching high,
And gave more light to north sundial clocks,
Whose gnomons tilted with the Earth's axis,
To point at the Sun from their hemisphere,
The blue planet's orbit traced an ellipse,
That made things hotter, while growing less near,
A paradox positively surpassed,
By the Sun's south pole showing Earth more shine,
But north and south often flipped in contrast,
To make an upside-down magnetic sign,
All of this gleamed in light eight minutes old,
Emitted by Earth's star that shone like gold.

A Sonnet for Triodos
The Ethical Bank

(Shakespearean sonnet and acrostic)

The Earth breathed deeply beneath windy hills,
Rain clouds flew, water fell, a river grew.
In swam fish, exchanging air through their gills,
On the banks, trees laid roots, drank in the view.
Displaying branches of thanks, their leaves sent
Oxygen back to the sky, where birds lungs
Sang songs to the Sun, and on each day went.
Each of those who gathered heard the winds tongues
Teaching how to plant and grow energy.
Harvests from sunshine, air and water fed
Into homes which built a community.
Collectively they aimed, they looked ahead,
At ways to work with nature, they all strived,
Laid foundations, where they and the Earth thrived.

*Scan this QRCode with your
smartphone to watch a recording
of this poem read by the author.*

Oceans Away
Washed Up During Lockdowns

(haiku)

The sea's bright blue waves
Beckon me to swim amongst
Oceans of face masks.

Cycling Round the West Country

(Cycle Poet Tour 2021)

I cycled around the West Country,
A bike bard on tour, performing my poetry,
I started at my local bike shop in Bristol,
Then onto Somerset,
Past a dragon sleeping in Worminster Hill.

I found an Albatross and an Ancient Mariner,
Saw Jupiter and Antares out being a stargazer,
I heard shanties sung on Watchet's sea shore,
Watched wagtails while camping up high on Exmoor.

The Lynton & Lynmouth railway took me up a clifftop,
That was a relief, looking down was a 500 ft drop,
In my cold tent, I made a blanket from an unfolded OS map,
Stayed in a B&B run by a Basil Fawlty,
Without the humour,
That was crap.

I found it hard to say goodbye to a statue of Tarka the Otter,
Was greeted to Lundy Island by a seal in the water,
A vandal seagull stole my porridge
And ripped a hole in my tent.
Then a shrew moved in,
I wanted to see wildlife,
But that wasn't what I meant.

I told poems in bikeshops, campsites, Coleridge's Cottage,
A ferry, and a village hall,
There was wind and rain, even fog, but also sunsets galore.
The story's not over, that was only part of my journey,
But I had quite the adventure,
Cycling round the West Country.

Upcycled No. 3
When Black Holes Become Stars

Some ancient civilisations believed,
That the blazing heavens could be perceived,
Through the pinpricked holes of a domed night sky,
The stars viewed differently in their mind's eye.
On my bit of Earth, 21st Century,
My black top's seeking haberdashery,
Also strewn with small holes, snagged and threadbare,
It's fifteen years old, in need of repair.
A needle turns black holes into gold stars,
Backstitching blue lines, maps out avatars,
Spelling out stories from mythology,
My top's adorned with Greek cosmology.
The tale of Queen Cassiopeia, vain,
Of cursed Medusa, by Perseus, slain,
And like Andromeda, saved from strife,
My old top's given a new lease of life.

It's Not Easy Being Green
A Poetry Diary: A Verse a Day for a Year

6
Do I buy what I need which is one loose lemon,
Or the organic four pack not pesticide sprayed,
On a black plastic tray wrapped in cellophane?
I opt for the single fruit in this conundrum.
It's not easy being green; did I get it right or wrong?

18
I'm confused by people alone in cars,
Getting angry at other people alone in cars.
People spinning in the gym have driven,
Riding a real bike reduces congestion.
It's not easy being green; but just cycle, walk, or run.

228
I never knew it was wrong to pick wildflowers,
They can't be tamed, indoors they won't survive,
The wildflowers' home is outdoors at all hours,
Under sun, stars and moon is where they thrive.
It's not easy being green; watch the flowers grow alive.

337
A coal mine's trying to open in Cumbria,
Near to St. Bees, a Heritage Coast area,
Sellafield Nuclear Waste Site's its other neighbour,
I thought crapping on your own doorstep was bad behaviour.
It's not easy being green;
Our 'leaders' do not care about being greener.

*367 verses were written in total (it was a leap year, and I wrote one extra due to being better at letters than counting). During lockdowns, I made 'It's Not Easy Being Green' into videos with guest speakers. The project was shown at Warrington Contemporary Arts Exhibition, and shortlisted for the Sustainability Art Prize.

The Only Way Out
is to Cycle through: Bereavements during the First Lockdown

(terza rima)

I pedalled out under a gloom ridden sky,
On a flat path haunted by ghosts of trees,
Their trunks, like a dead giant's ribcage, twisted high.

Winds tore through those bones in bitter eddies,
A crumbling skin of leaves littered the trail, numbed,
I cycled on, past those shadowy sentries.

I pedalled, met by clouds heavy with hail,
On the same path, the trees had mummified,
Each shrivelled branch pointing with a stubbed fingernail.

Ice hammered wood, out of sync, amplified,
The path was pelted as if detested,
I cycled past those clashing drummers, petrified.

I pedalled beneath clouds filled with a flood,
On the path, the trees stood over their graves,
Like bloated corpses that had ruptured, smeared with mud.

Murky sobs streaked down the trees in runged staves,
Trying to bandage the trunks with their grief,
Bogged down, I cycled through the path's sludge filled concaves.

Spears tipped the branches, all bared like sharp teeth,
I rode and I rode, I wanted relief,
But saw each thorn wrapped in a scaled-down wreath.

I pedalled to the sun in disbelief,
On the path, the trees were resurrected,
Waving hello breezily with each fresh green leaf.

Their branches formed a shelter overhead,
On the flat path, shadows, and light shone through,
Making the shape of a ladder which led,
Me and my bike up, out into a brighter view.

Solar Sonnet 12
Ruling Bodies

Is the Sun similar to a monarch?
It rules a system; even has a crown,
Its planets are pulled in circles, starstruck,
Kept distant but bound, sun-up or sun-down,
But even great Suns all age, they lose strength,
With less gravity, the planets then stray,
On orbital paths of increasing length,
They wander, but don't quite go their own way,
'Til the Sun transforms into a giant,
Its bloated red face gobbles worlds and more,
Then it seems like a corrupt government,
Full of toxic hot air at its shrunken core,
Even denser is its final decline,
A white star so dim it can't even shine.

#MeToo, #MeNeither

Six characters joined to gain momentum,
A hashtag connecting women worldwide.
"Are you a solution, or part of the problem?"
A male zealot rants I must pick a side
For the cause, pressurising those unable
To like, share, retweet, to add their own name.
It's all well and good being stuck with a label,
But not if it adds trauma on those not to blame.

Pass it on!

I watch in awe as Rose blossoms with rage,
While moguls pretending to hear close their ears.
The spotlight on trouble off screen and off stage
Has investors' blind eyes peeking out of fear
At zero returns on heroes. Their products placed
Get redeveloped into parts to be played
About the reformed: "He's grown, no longer disgraced,"
And the victims bear witness to this shit-parade.

Pass it on.

I fume about a heartless reporter
Chasing news headlines as I watch aghast,
When she accosts Uma on camera
For a soundbite with subtext that asks:
If it happened to her, or if she escaped?
Tell me, when did it become okay
To ask someone if they've ever been... ?
It's a word I find too difficult to say.

Pass it on?

This pours out of me, sat opposite my friend,
Our knees touching under a café table.
Caught in a conversation with no happy end,
I realise too late my mistake. It's painful.
Tears threaten her eyes, so beautifully sad.
Meaning's understood in what's left unsaid.
"I can't," she whispers; a small shake of her head.
She stares at her mug, a cold cup of tea.
"Me, neither," I murmur, blinking rapidly.

We let it pass.

Tomato
For Female Reproductive Rights

(haiku)

To martyr? To mate?
To veg out, or be fruitful?
My cherry. My choice!

The Hawthorn

(Petrarchan sonnet)

A native bush from the North, the Hawthorn,
When grown in the right hemisphere you'll find,
It sometimes has the power to spellbind
Lost hearts drifting over the wilds, forlorn.
One bush stands fast, on a fell weather worn,
Thriving, despite the elements that grind.
Its barbed branches catch me. I become entwined.
The thorns pierce my skin. My feathers are torn.
Deep within, the bush's heart is ablaze,
I peck the thorns out, flick them on the fire,
The flames form a song-thrush: wings scratched and grazed.
We heal our wounds, cooing with desire,
Feed each other berries, gather white bouquets,
And make our nest in the Hawthorn briar.

The Last Waltz

The courting lovebirds danced,
He pushed forwards, entranced.
Forced her one step behind,
His leading turned her blind.
He made moves she sidestepped,
Held too tight; she felt kept.

Feet unswept, she flew:
                              freestyle.

Disenchanted in Narnia

(Shakespearean sonnet)

A lamppost dimmed by a nevergreen tree,
Where no one waited, not even Tumnus.
I had left a faded festivity,
A cold place that could never be Christmas.

I hid in church shadows, but dead trees spied,
No saviour for me, the Lion long gone,
I drunk myself numb, as my own light died,
Amongst graves laid flat, stone tables for one.

"I'm here," his voice crept, a warm-blooded sound,
With black spells, the White Witch came in disguise,
To claim a sacrifice, so I was bound,
With sweet words I swallowed, all laced with lies
That froze me with the statues where I stood,
In a graveyard, near a lamp, by a wood.

The Empty Gesture

(katauta)

He filled a giftbox
With empty apologies,
Like an incomplete poem -

31

Cycling the Outer Hebrides

(Burns stanza)

Barra, Eriskay, South Uist:
Is where roads wove for this cyclist,
To see a Sea Rocket exist:
That mauve cracker.
Beaches sown by a wild florist,
On the *machair*.

From Culla Bay's beach, I watched flow,
From land to water – a rainbow,
The Western sky was set aglow
With that crown.
Then, the sea took one long swallow,
Drank the arch down.

If I were a mushroom, I'd root
Myself on land, where I can shoot,
Near the sea, with sunshine to boot,
And spend my day
Growing up, bearing fungi fruit,
On Vatersay.

I've been for a ride, not a race,
With wind, rain, and sun changing pace,
Stopped at many a passing place,
For a breather.
The Hebrides is a top space,
That is Outer.

What Grows Well beside that Willow?

What grows well beside that Willow?
Not the insincere charm,
Meaning well, doing harm,
Of the Yew tree's encroaching bane.

What grows well beside that Willow?
Not darling buds entwined,
Round a wreath barbed and spined,
Bound in the Hawthorn's piercing spell.

What grows well beside that Willow?
Not Mahonia's gold tongue,
Gifting sprigs, coldly sprung,
Disguised as summer's Laburnum.

The Willow is elemental,
In so many ways,
With air and water it plays,
Earth softens to its rooting touch.

Would the heart-shaped leaves of the Lime
Renew their vows each spring?
Would the Oak gift one ring?
The Larch promise to stay evergreen?

Can no other tree grow beside
The Willow as it weaves
Its heart upon its leaves,
That turn silver to gold when they fall?

That Willow, so elemental,
In all but one way,
Grows fast, is faster slain,
Felled by its own flame when it loves.

Poetry-itis

Before I ever studied poetry,
My brain played a song on repetition,
Which, when cycling, I'd hear relentlessly:
'The Going Gets Tough' by Billy Ocean.
Then, I did English Lit for my degree,
And naively thought Ozzy meant Osbourne,
But there are works much more insidious,
Even dead, Shelley can ruin a woman.
So what it was written by a Romantic!
Who'd want the earworm Ozymandias?
Eighties pop overthrown by a classic;
No longer Billy's 'Tough' tune 'Gets Going'.
I ride with pentameters iambic,
In cycling rhymes, I can't stop composing.

Banana Bike Rockets

I'm out on my bike, bananas in my back pockets,
Potassium propelling my pedals uphill.
Friendly shells containing yellow-green rockets,
Healthy fuel for when this cyclist needs to refill.
Leave no 'nana behind if they get mashed out on duty,
Back home at base camp, blitz them into a smoothie.

If My Heart was My Bicycle

(ballad)

If my heart was my bicycle,
I wouldn't give it away,
I would leave it with those I trust
Care for it, the right way.
It's precious and needs safe-keeping,
My bike, I'd not mislay.

If my bike has to wait outside,
I lock it somewhere bright,
It doesn't feel left out in the cold
With other bikes in sight.
My bike's quite a sociable soul,
When conditions are right.

But, it knows the key combination,
Hearts get weighed down by locks,
Chains misused to shackle free-will:
They're romantic roadblocks.
Freewheels spin links which pull together,
Bikes get this paradox.

My bike avoids certain terrains,
Rocky roads are too rough,
They'll upend a cyclist quick as ice:
That smooth, slick, nasty stuff.
If my bike goes down suspect roads,
It knows when is enough.

You see, my bike has traversed frontiers,
But respects boundaries,
When others choose to run red lights,
Those warning signs it sees.
My bike's not thrown off-balance by
Bad bearings such as these.

Good wheels are the ones which stay true,
My bike accepts no less,
Loose spokes warp, twist and dissemble,
Despite what they profess.
It steers clear of too much tension seeking,
Spokes snap from excess stress.

Disconnected bolts which rattle,
Or squeaking rusty chains,
Need acknowledgement, not neglect,
When a component complains.
A happy bike sings harmonies,
With finely tuned refrains.

So, if Cupid's errant arrows pierce
Tyres with his bad aims,
I'll now fix flats and ride away
Far from his funless games.
Tyres filled with breaths of fresh air;
They support both our frames.

I'll apply all this bike psychology,
Next time love tries to strike,
It shows my mind, body and soul,
What real love should feel like.
I'll know who's right to share life's cycles with,
If I treat my heart like my bike.

The Bristol Bike Bard

Verse 90: St. Mary's Churchyard. BS16.

In winter, Hades' Underworld is home for Persephone,
But when she returns to earth in spring, snowdrops appear,
My bike and I saw she'd passed through
                             the churchyard of St. Mary.

Verse 102: Mars, Kingswood Park. BS15.

On my bike, I found directions to Mars in Kingswood Park,
A sign points to the planet. An asteroid's up there, too,
It's named 'Pillinger', after Colin, a bright science spark.

Verse 119: The Corn Exchange, Corn Street. BS1.

Time used to be set when true high-noon occurred naturally,
Bristol's sun climbs the sky eleven minutes after London's,
Corn Street's clock tells both times; one hand ticks locally.

Verse 123: Super Pink Full Moon, Bristol, Earth.

The Pink Full Moon was named where Native Americans stood,
From my bike, I watched *księżyc, dayax, yuèliàng, luna* rise,
That's some of its names in Bristol's part of the planethood.

Verse 133: Cheers Drive, Speedwell. BS5

There is a street in Bristol where local humour combines
With a phrase people say when getting off the bus,
Folks voted to name this street: "Cheers Drive",
                             one of life's great signs.

*All 180 terza rima verses began as a way to help me leave the house for local rides during lockdown to alleviate depression. They ended up on Adam Crowther's BBC Radio Bristol Upload shows, BBC Radio 4's 'Sketches' arts programme, covered by Bristol Cycling Campaign, Bristol 24/7, Bristol Life Magazine, and made into a documentary 'Bristol Bike Bard' by Dave MacFarlane, which was shown at Kendal Mountain, Sheffield Adventure, Adventure Uncovered Film Festivals.

Solar Sonnet 14
The Summer Solstice

Like the Solstice, I'm extremely inclined,
Towards the Sun on Earth's longest of days,
From its north-east point where it was assigned,
To start Summer's highest climb, beaming rays,
Above the stone circle at Stanton Drew,
The waning gibbous moon watched the Sun rise,
Venus had raced south, but Jupiter flew
High in the blue, as dawn painted pink skies,
Earth turned anti-clockwise; we danced sunwise,
Planets and people all twirled for the Sun,
Such beautiful light, a sight for sore eyes,
At quarter to five on the horizon.
After midsummer, nights start drawing in,
One cycle ends, another can begin.

Appendix: Glossary of Poetic Forms

(haibun)

Acrostic: The first letter of each line read vertically downwards form a word or message. Can make poets feel like secret agents.

Ballad: Often about love, usually in quatrains, sometimes six-line stanzas as in Oscar Wilde's 'Ballad of Reading Gaol'.

Blank Verse/Heroic Verse: 10 syllables/iambic pentameter, of unrhymed lines, as in Wordsworth's 'Tintern Abbey'.

Burns Stanza: Six short lines. Lines 1, 2, 3 & 5 rhyme with 8 syllables, 4 & 6 rhyme with four syllables. Made famous by Robert Burns, but first written by Robert Sempill in 'Lament for Habbie Simpson': a piper from a village where I went to school for a while, and which never shared this fact even when teaching Burns.

Free Verse: The form that does whatever it wants as long as it flows. Certain trends pit free verse against form, which is like pitting Soundgarden against Glenn Miller. Both are great.

Haibun: Japanese form created by Basho, which combines prose and Haiku, a bit like this appendix, in an ironic, post-modernist kind of way.

Haiku: Japanese form of 3 lines, syllables 5,7,5. Traditionally nature themed.

The form's been embraced
Although the theme hasn't been
I hold my hands up.

Katauta: Japanese form. 3 lines, 5, 7, 7 syllables. Stanzas create a call and response between lovers. When unanswered, it's a katuata. If responded to it becomes a **sedōka.**

Kyrielle: Originally stemming from the Christian prayer: Kyrie Eleison. Quatrains have a last line refrain. Often misheard as a love interest's name in the 80s song by Mr. Mister.

Luc Bat: Vietnamese form. Lines alternate six and eight syllables, with the last sixth syllable rhyming with the sixth syllable on the next eight syllabled line, changing to a new rhyming pair throughout.

Pantoum: Malaysian form which has evolved into quatrains with repeating lines. Lines 2 & 4 become lines 3 & 1 in the next stanza. The final verse's second & fourth lines repeat the first stanza's first and third lines.

Petrarchan Sonnet: 14 lines, iambic pentameter. The first 8 lines often develop an idea, which turns in the last 6 lines. Much easier if writing in Italian. Choose your unruly English end rhymes wisely.

Rhyming Couplets: Paired lines that rhyme. Utilised by tired cyclists writing poems when touring a show across the country.

Sestina: Six stanzas, six lines each, with the end words repeating in different orders in the consecutive stanzas, topped off with a three-line envoi which includes all six words. If you can crack this, you are a secret agent.

Shakespearean Sonnet: As with the Burns Stanza, not created by, but popularised by its namesake. 14 lines, three individual quatrains and a rhyming couplet. In iambic pentameter.

Spenserian Stanza: 9 lines, 8 in iambic pentameter, ending with a ninth in iambic hexameter.

Spenserian Sonnet: 14 lines, iambic pentameter, in quatrains linking in rhymes, ending in a couplet. Again, choose end words with care.

Terza Rima: Three lines with end rhymes forming a chain with the stanzas before and after, ending with a four lined stanza. Dante probably holds the record with over 4,700 stanzas in *The Divine Comedy*.

Villanelle: Yes, an unhinged TV secret agent, but also a form possibly developed by one. Five stanzas, three lines each. The first and third lines of the first stanza alternate through the remaining verses, and form the final rhyming couplet. Hopefully it makes some kind of sense, unless it is a coded message by MI6.

Biography

Caroline Burrows' poetry has appeared on BBC Radio 4, BBC Radio Bristol, in BBC Sky at Night Magazine, the Charles Causley Trust, Sinew: 10 Years of Poetry in the Brew, First Flight: Paper Cranes Anthology, Morecambe Poetry Festival Anthology, and the Wilfred Owen Association Journal amongst others. She has also been Poet in Residence at Cromarty Arts Trust.

Her year of daily video eco-verses project: 'It's Not Easy Being Green' was short-listed for the Sustainability First Art Prize. The documentary, 'Bristol Bike Bard', by Dave MacFarlane/DMTwo Media, showed Caroline exploring her local area during lockdown to help manage her mental health, and was officially selected for Kendal Mountain Film Festival.

She has written commissions for Glenside Hospital Museum, Bristol Ideas, and Triodos: The Ethical Bank. She toured her 'Turning Pedals into Poems' show by bicycle in an eco-friendly, low-carbon, heavy-panniered way, with the show being Saboteur Awards shortlisted, and her efforts having Caroline named one of Cycling UK's #100WomenInCycling.

Caroline's flash fiction pieces have been published in the National Flash Fiction Anthology, Charles Causley Trust, and Lancaster One-Minute Monologues. Her articles about her literary themed cycling adventures are in Cycle, and Adventure Cyclist Magazines, as well as literary/astronomy crossover articles in BBC Sky at Night Magazine. She gives talks about her adventures and has been a regular speaker at the Cycle Touring Festival.

Caroline has an MA in Creative Writing and teaches poetry/creative writing workshops.

Social media: @VerseCycle

Other titles are available from

The Jawbone Collective, Lexical Ninjas and *Wessex Media*

The Jawbone Collective: is a micro publisher and social enterprise created as a not for profit organisation for furthering the literary arts in the South-West region. Established in 2019, *The Jawbone Collective* is a Community Interest Company run by a group of South-West writers. *The Jawbone Collective* was founded on the idea of building confidence in creatives to help enable them celebrate and share their work with a wider audience through publication and performance of their collections or pamphlets in print and digital mediums. All money raised by the author on their copies is theirs to keep. All money raised in book sales by the publisher is returned to the collective to underwrite publication of future writers.

We believe that poets can 'emerge' at any age and believe the quality of our Author's work speaks for itself. Each poet we have published has gained confidence and used their books to finance and promote their craft. Every writer has contributed to events in their own area and gone on to establish other events, be commissioned to produce work, promote work through other mediums, and establish themselves through competitions, slams and public broadcast.

It costs approximately £800 to bring a new writer from our initial approach through to final publication. *The Jawbone Collective* was established and backed by our principal editor and founder Peter Roe. The continuance of this project is dependent on the support of Creative Members by donations of Time, Soft Skills and Talents. Book Sales, Donations, Sponsorship, Grants and Bursaries from Businesses and Arts Organisations.

Please consider a donation to help publish emerging poets.
You can follow this QR Code with your smartphone.
Payment can be via Apple or Google Pay or with a bank card.

Lexical Ninjas: was established to publish more experienced poets across the UK on a cooperative, open and transparent publication basis. Members of The Jawbone Collective skill share their artistic, editorial and production talents to help produce the books and all profits are returned to the collective. Although these are author-paid publications, we apply the same high standards to selecting work and bringing the author to publication. We work with the author to edit, design and layout their book. The production schedule and all costs are established from the start, an 'open book' that helps to underwrite publication of emerging writers.

To enquire about a cooperative publication **email** to **lexicalninjas@wessex.media**

If you are an Arts or community organisation interested in hosting or sponsoring a creative writing workshop or an outdoor or indoor poetry or spoken word event please call our **Managing Editor**, *Peter Roe* on: **0787 659 6184**

www.wessex.media